LOVE, LIFE
AND
LAUGHTER
POEMS FOR CHILDREN

Zoe Karl

Copyright © 2012 Zoe Karl

All rights reserved.

ISBN:1479218332
ISBN-13:9781479218332

i

Ingredients for this book

- Carefully place one child with a passion for poetry in a large room.
- Add in a pinch of writing utensils and a large dollop of paper.
- Mix together with lots of imagination, curiosity, inspiration and eagerness to learn.
- Then leave to cool for a few minutes before adding loads of fun and friendship to help with final ideas.
- Lastly serve with a front cover, blurb and pictures so the presentation and contents are equally pleasing. Enjoy!

Love, Life and Laughter

MODERN AND ORIGINAL POEMS
WRITTEN FOR CHILDREN BY A CHILD

Zoe Karl

CONTENTS

Acknowledgments

WINTER
Sledging	Page 2
Snowy Day	Page 3
Christmas	Page 4
Rain	Page 5
The Frozen Forest	Page 6

HAIKU
Haiku, Haiku	Page 7
Mum Haiku	Page 7
Erosion Haiku	Page 7

SPRING AND SUMMER
Summers Day	Page 8
Summer Sun	Page 8
Spring Flowers	Page 9
Garden Beauty	Page 9

LIFE, FEELINGS & EMOTIONS
I Love:	Page 10
Happy	Page 10
You	Page 11
For My Mum	Page 11
Babies	Page 12
Birth	Page 12
Why?	Page 13
It will be OK	Page 13
That's Life	Page 14
Laughter	Page 14

NATURE AND ANIMALS

Waves	Page 15
Light	Page 15
Mr Oak	Page 16
Cliffs	Page 17
Nature's Day	Page 17
Little Birds	Page 18
The Horse, the Dog and the Cat	Page 18

FOOD

Pie	Page 19
Perfect Packets	Page 20
Clementine, Tangerine, Satsuma	Page 20

SIMILIES AND METAPHORS

Similies and Metaphors	Page 21

MUSIC AND DANCE

Feel the rhythm	Page 22
The Dancer	Page 22
Elegance	Page 23

POEMS FOR OLDER CHILDREN

The Valley of Violence	Page 24
Mountains of Malice	Page 24
Go to Bed!	Page 25
Effortless Wanderer	Page 26

ALLSORTS

Nonsense Poem	Page 27
Dump	Page 28
Books	Page 29
Candle	Page 29
Soldiers	Page 29
Hair	Page 30
Hats	Page 30
Unexplainable	Page 31
Scarecrow	Page 31

Zoe Karl

ACKNOWLEDGMENTS

Pictures from Microsoft Clipart and Google Images have been used in this publication. Thanks to Maia for her help in Nonsense poem and Grace in Valley of Violence. Thanks to Forest Row C.E Primary School for teaching and inspiring me. Finally to my Mum and Dad for supporting me.

Love, Life and Laughter

WINTER

Sledging

Whooshing down at quite a speed,
Warm clothes and a sledge are all you need,

To have tons of fun in the snow,
There's no chance we'll go slow.

First the big run, then the small,
Then the thin one, then the tall.

Such a steep run at a height,
Gosh it gave us both a fright.

Can't see anything, ice in my eyes,
Every single bump - a surprise.

My hands are frozen, but thanks to my mum,
She lends me her gloves, now she'll get numb!

But now it's time to go back to the apartment,
We'll come back tomorrow to sledge the steep
descent!

*

Snowy Day

When I wake up I rub my eyes twice
All the water's now frozen ice
Trees laden with glistening snow
Boots trudging, heavily moving, slow
Happy faces all around
Screams of laughter; the only sound
It's fallen 2 feet at least or more
Everyone is chilled to the core
Then come inside and drink a cocoa
Warm by the fire till it's time to go
Snuggle in bed and drift away
Lie and wait for the next snowy day!

*

Christmas

Cottages topped with glistening snow
Santa chuckling ho, ho, ho
Evergreens decorated with dazzling light
Little robin red breast taking flight
Colourfully wrapped presents topped with bows
Rudolf the friendly reindeer with a bright red nose
A pretty wreath hanging on the door
Carol singers singing until their throats are sore
Happy Mr Snowman with his top hat
Church bells ringing, nativity's performing, how about that
And when Christmas day has finally come
We shall sing around the piano, share gifts and have fun!

Rain

Rain is thudding heavily
Resting on the ground
I can't get a moments peace
With the persistent, rhythmical sound
The trees are swaying viciously
The sky is angry, grey
With the water it's hard to see
Hard to find my way.

*

The Frozen Forest

A soft crunching is heard underfoot as I walk
Glistening snow glimmers as white as chalk
We stride along taking our time
The Ashdown Forest is sublime
The scenery's lovely, the scent is great
To explore, I just can't wait
You take my hand, we share a smile
I gaze in your eyes for a while

A stream approaches, frozen with ice
You help me over you're kind and nice
We laugh and have a snowball fight
The forest view is such a sight
The end of our trip is drawing near
As you gently whisper something in my ear
My heart fills up with joy, I'm over the moon
We depart but will be back again soon…

*

HAIKU

Haiku, Haiku

This is a Haiku
Do you like to read haiku's?
They are very short.

*

Mum Haiku

I love my mummy
She helps me in all I do
So pretty she is.

*

Erosion Haiku

Undercuts erode
Then turn into larger caves
Which change to stacks

*

SPRING AND SUMMER

Summers Day (aged 8)

On a summers day
Lying on the ground
It is very sunny
And there's not a sound
But the trees that whistle
And the birds that tweet
There's a kitten playing
Isn't that SWEET!

*

Summer Sun (aged 8)

As I sit in my garden with my kitten on my lap,
On a heavy wooden bench,
What I see is flowers swaying in the wind,
Oh the beauty of this season,
Splashing giggling getting wet,
Can you guess what it is?
Of course, it is a paddling pool,
Have an ice cream nice and cool.

*

Spring Flowers

Flowers the colours of yellow and white
Sitting proudly radiant and bright
When spring comes they blossom and bloom
Sharing their delicate, sweet perfume.

(For Mrs Galea Spring 2012)

*

Garden Beauty

Daffodil, aster, forget me not
These flowers we do love a lot
The colours are yellow and red and blue
Give them for presents for love that is true.

*

LIFE, FEELINGS & EMOTIONS

I love:
Dancing, singing, walking,
Acting, playing, talking,
Maths, English, reading,
On the motorway speeding (Shh!)
Cooking, football kicking,
Yummy ice cream licking,
Fresh strawberry picking,
Watching clocks ticking,
Brother's sweets nicking!
I love all these things. What do you love?

*

Happy

Emotion, feeling an important part of life
Helps you oh so greatly when you're going through strife
If someone's struggling to be happy, give them a laugh or a smile
They can build up happiness, one brick then one tile
Until they reach the summit and are as happy as can be
They might even be as joyful as you and me!

You

Like yourself whoever you are
Because from yourself you are never far
So when no one's caring and you need someone there
Just think 'I'm always there for me,
I will always care.'

*

For my mum when I was going to New York
March 2012

Do not be sad and don't be blue
I'll be back in four days – to cuddle you
I'll miss you and you'll miss me
But smile and try to be happy
What's four days in the great scheme of things?
Just think of Easter and the joy it brings
I'll have a great time and so will you
Nothing parts our love, fair and true!

Babies

Babies make such fusses over things
I think they should be banned
I'd be so much happier
If there was nothing in Jeff's pram!

*

Birth

In your life you'll get the chance to have a little baby
Yes, no, which one to choose, for now let's just say maybe
The good parts are they're cutie pies for which you care and love
The bad parts are the sleepless nights with the moon shining above
The greatest day in my opinion is when they say a word
Whether it's mamma, papa, red or blue
It's so sweet to be heard.

Why?

Why is there such thing as illness?
Why is there such thing as sores?
Why is there such thing as heartbreak?
Why is there such thing as bores?

Is it because of Pandora?
Or is it Adam and Eve
Or is the because of the snake
That said eat the apple
What do you believe?

Why isn't everyone happy
Why doesn't everyone laugh?
Why doesn't everyone smile when a teacher says
add up 2 and a half?

*

It will be Ok - after my grandfather's death when
I was 9

When a relative dies, it will always bring sadness
But after the funeral
It will always bring gladness
At the funeral it will be ok
You should have a good cry
This is a little poem about when people die

That's life

There's always a star in heaven
There's always love in my heart
There's always friendship between us
And home is a good place to start
The sun is always shining
The moon is always bright
That's the sign that it's night time
So it's time to say good night.

*

Laughter

A snort, a giggle, through your teeth,
A raucous burst, a snigger,
And when someone tells a joke,
They get louder and bigger and bigger.

*

NATURE AND ANIMALS

Waves

Hissing, fizzing you hear her moan
Screeching in her high pitched tone
Scooping you up in her massive hands
She forces you down to her murky sands
Can you escape? You just try!
She's mean, clever, cunning and sly,
Her minions in the form of sea creatures
With powers and many fascinating features
You'll feel her wrath if you go to her domain
The sea is incredible – she really does reign.

*

Light

Illuminates your way
Inspires and discovers
Great to help you see
Trustworthy light

*

Mr Oak

He stands his ground through hot and cold
Rooted firmly big and bold
Swishing his arms elegantly
Munching squirrels for his tea
As they clamber his almighty trunk
He swallows his prey in one large chunk
More vulnerable is he when the winds do blow
The perfectly formed green leaves slowly go
But never beaten, he remains
Through thick and thin he never complains
If you whisper to him, he'll keep your words
To tell a secret is quite absurd
His generosity does always show
Hopefully it will never go
He keeps young birds on his arms
And keeps them safe from natures harms
The forest love him, it's plain to see
That love is also shared by me
His whispering you sometimes hear
Then you'll know that he is near.

Cliffs

Cliffs erode after many years
Lighthouse nearby and some piers
In the sea there are lots of fish
Freely wonder if you wish
Fine sand lays on the ground
Seagulls make a screechy sound!

*

Natures Day

Boats glide along the sleeping sea
Trees as harmonious as can be
The bright sun burns down on my face
It is such a peaceful place
The sky is a beautiful blue
I like to admire the stunning view

The clouds float very high and still
There's a chirpy bird above the hill
I lay back in the fine, thin sand
The tree branch like a crooked hand
In the distance I see a glint of gold
As if a mystery's about to unfold.

*

Little Birds

In a little nest
With their little beaks
First chick flies away
To find out what she seeks

Mummy brings a worm
Yummy, very good
They have a lovely time
Doing what birds should

They grow into big birds
And they learn to fly
They glide and soar into the air
Going very high

*

The Horse the Dog and the Cat

The horse, the dog and the cat,
Altogether now how about that!
The horse said aloud,
And then he meowed!
'I like dog's lovely new hat.'

*

FOOD

Pie

As I walk in the door I pick up the scent
Oh, I wouldn't give this dish up for lent
Creep to the oven, take a peek
The most beautiful pie, my eyes do seek

The crust is golden, gives off a shine
I hope the biggest piece is mine.

A luxurious crunch! A burst of senses!
Lick my lips as the cooking commences
Finally it's time to eat the treat
But no great pie is complete….
Without a fork, a knife, a spoon
Eat it all up and hope for another one soon!

Perfect Packets

Crunch
Crack
Lip smack
Every flavour
Just savour
Peppery
Salty
No crisps faulty
Pick
Choose
Nothing to loose
Every crisp is nice
You have to eat them twice!

*

Clementine, Tangerine, Satsuma,
Which is best to fill my hunger?
No one knows the difference, no one
ever will,
They're all ripe and juicy and they all taste brill!

SIMILIES AND METAPHORS

Smiles and metaphors in writing, really open doors.

For similes use like and as
To describe the properties something has
For example "she's like a raging bull"
Similes are so simple
Or there are metaphors, they're simple too
Just say "she is a raging bull"
That's all you need to do

So similes say something's like but metaphors say it is,
That is all you need to know, so don't get in a tiz!

*

MUSIC AND DANCE

Feel the Rhythm

Strum, strum, bang, bang,
Twist, twist, twang, twang,
Keep to the beat
Tap your feet
Rhythm and groove
Play it smooth
Treble clef and bass
Along with the pace
Clear some space
Make music today
Come and play!

*

The Dancer

Twirling and swirling all day long
Looking so great with their costume on
Dancing gracefully and so smooth
I'd love to be a dancer
Wouldn't You?

*

Elegance

Floating in the air like a fairy leaping
From leg to leg jumping to the sky
As high as high, pointing your toes
As flexed as they can go
Imagining yourself on a stage

*

POEMS FOR OLDER CHILDREN

The Valley of Violence

In the valley of violence
The streets are stained with blood
The trees spiky branches hang down and
Scratch anyone who dares go by like
Claws catching their prey
Anonymous hands reach out and grab at
You as you walk down the cobbled path
Citizens stay in their houses so as not
To get attacked by blood thirsty strangers
Lurking in the shadows
Those who dare to enter can be assured never to
return…..

*

Mountains of Malice

In the mountains of malice
The houses are as dark as midnight
The stones on the windy path scowl up at you
All the people stricken with hatred, choose to be
lonely
Like clouds floating alone in a stormy sky
Snow thuds to the ground as if to punish
everyone who dares live there.

Go to Bed!

M = Mum
J = son James

M: Go to bed darling
J: No way, I've done my homework, now it's time to play
M: Oh come on James, don't be naughty
J: Alright, alright, don't get haughty
M: Ok, I'm sorry – just it's late
J: But dad's not back yet, can't I wait?
M: It's a school night and you need your sleep
J: Just give me an hour, I'll be dreaming deep
M: An hours too long – how about a half?
J: Half's not long enough – don't make me laugh
M:5 minutes
J:25
M:10
J:20
M:12
J:19
M: 15, James that's plenty
J: No it's not – you don't understand
M: One minute's fine then – it's more than I planned
J: Fine then if that's how you're gonna be

M: Oh James, it's because I care you see (time passes)
M: Right, one minute's up, time to go upstairs
J: Not fair mum, I'm in the middle of pairs
M: You, young man will …..
J: Just get lost (shouts)
M: Gracious me, that rudeness will cost – enough is enough now go to bed
J: Fine, whatever, I'll do what you said.

*

Effortless Wanderer

Always. Always look at the eyes. The eyes that blink, the eyes that wink, the eyes that sing silently. The eyes that flutter, the eyes that flash, the eyes that dance so energetically but still.
The eyes that are the window to your soul, the eyes that give the game away, the eyes that guide you. The eyes that reveal the truth, the eyes that effortlessly wander, the eyes that love and laugh and live.
Always. Always look at the eyes.

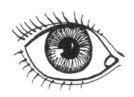

ALLSORTS

Nonsense Poem

There are stars in the sky
And there's rain pouring down
There's a hair in my eye
But there's no hair to be found

There's a hat on my head
But I can't afford clothes
There's a boy from my school
But I don't go to school – everyone knows…

There's a swing in my garden
But it's just a patio
There's a beat in my chest
But I died long ago

I said I had a house
But I am long dead
I want to go to sleep
But I don't have a head

*

Zoe Karl

Dump

At the dump
There's so much

Broken toys
Things for boys

Rotting fruit
A rusty flute

Old bicycles
A jar of pickles

Water bottles
Wrecked car throttles

Ripped up posters
Roller coasters

Dad went to get rid of some things
But came back with more!!

*

Books

My teacher says books are good for the
imagination
I completely disagree
If I had the choice
I'd break them!

*

Candle

Strike a match
Light the wick
Burn it down
Melting quick

*

Soldiers

1,2,3 1,2,3 come on soldiers
come with me
We are training to be the
best
I wonder where we'll be
fighting next?
1,2,3 1,2,3 come on soldiers,
come with me.

Hair

Blond, brown, ginger, black
Soft, rough, silky, tough
Curly, straight, wavy, grey
Which one is yours today?

Hats

Beanies, bobbles, top hats too
There are hats for all, even me and you
All unique, wear them with pride
Which one to choose – you decide
Black, blue, orange, pink
White, grey, purple, mink
Every single hat makes me smile
Whether for warmth
Or just for style!

*

Unexplainable

Things happen,
That you can't name
Some things
You just can't explain

*

Scarecrow

In a field, far away,
Stands a figure in the hay,
Take a peek, a closer look,
Across the field, right to the brook.
A pasty face, a gentle smile,
The farmer's time was spent worthwhile,
Dungarees too large to fit,
A blue, brimmed hat that's torn and split.
And when the moon's arisen high,
He sleeps under the vast night sky.

*

Dear Reader
I would like to inform you of some very exciting
news – please pick up a pen in your right or left
hand and place a piece of paper in front of you.
Now you can write your own poem, it cost's no
money but cost's lots of time. It will be worth it in
the end – all you need to do is rhyme!
Yours Thankfully (and keep writing!)
Zoe

*****

ABOUT THE AUTHOR

Photo: Chris Hall

Zoe Karl was born in 2000 and lives in East Sussex with her Mum, Dad, Brother and their 2 cats. Zoe has loved writing poetry since she was 6 year's old and also has a passion for dancing, acting and singing.

Made in the USA
Charleston, SC
12 November 2012